FRIEND POWER

HOW THE FRIENDS YOU CHOOSE CAN CHANGE THE COURSE OF YOUR LIFE

By
STEPHANIE SCHELLER

Dedication:

This book is dedicated to all the aspiring souls out there who are struggling to achieve their ultimate success in life and willing to take any steps necessary to make that happen!

Copyright ©2015 Stephanie Scheller
All rights reserved. Written permission must be secured from the publisher to use or reproduce any part of this book, except for brief quotations in critical reviews or articles.

This publication is designed to provide accurate and authoritative information in regard to the subject matter covered. It is sold with the understanding that the publisher is not engaged in rendering legal, accounting, or other professional service. If legal advice or other expert assistance is required, the services of a professional should be sought.

Scheller, Stephanie
Friend Power: How the Friends You Choose Can Change the Course of Your Life
ISBN: 978-0-9962288-0-0

Contents

AESOP'S FABLE: THE ASS & HIS PURCHASER.......	5
ACKNOWLEDGEMENTS..	7
FOREWORD BY ANNA SCHELLER.......................	9
CHAPTER 1: INTRODUCTIONS...........................	13
CHAPTER 2: THE EVERYMAN MOLD..................	19
CHAPTER 3: WHAT IS ULTIMATE SUCCESS?...........	23
CHAPTER 4: FRIEND POWER DEFINED...............	27
CHAPTER 5: ACTION TAKERS V. ACTION TALKERS..	31
CHAPTER 6: FRIENDS PAVE YOUR CAREER..........	35
CHAPTER 7: BECOMING FINANCIALLY FREE........	41
CHAPTER 8: FRIENDS & FITNESS.......................	45
CHAPTER 9: THE KEY TO SPIRITUALITY..............	47
CHAPTER 10: FAMILY LIFE & FRIEND POWER......	51
CHAPTER 11: STUNT OR SUPPORT YOUR PERSONAL GROWTH...	55
CHAPTER 12: EMOTIONAL HANDLING: HEALTHY OR HURTING...	59
CHAPTER 13: STARVING ARTISTS WANT TO BE STARVING ARTISTS...	63
CHAPTER 14: THE PASSIONIST V. THE HOBBIEST..	67
CHAPTER 15: ATHLETIC SUPERIORITY ISN'T EVERYTHING..	73
CHAPTER 16: VICTIMS ARE VICTIMS.................	77
CHAPTER 17: HOW TO LEVERAGE FRIEND POWER...	81
CHAPTER 18: CONCLUSIONS...........................	87
MY READING MATERIAL.................................	91
ABOUT THE AUTHOR.....................................	93

The Ass & His Purchaser
From Aesop's Fables

A man wished to purchase an Ass (a Donkey), and decided to give the animal a test before buying him. He took the Ass home and put him in the field with his other Asses.

The new Ass strayed from the others to join the one that was the laziest and the biggest eater of them all.

Seeing this, the man led him back to his owner. When the owner asked how he could have tested the Ass in such a short time, the man answered, "I didn't even need to see how he worked. I knew he would be just like the one he chose to be his friend."

Acknowledgements

First I feel that I need to acknowledge my Mom for always encouraging me, always believing in me, and never giving up on me. She is my inspiration and I'm proud to know her, work with her, encourage her and see where we will go together!

I also need to thank Matthew for being my rock, holding me steady, always believing in me, encouraging me, keeping my nose to the grindstone when I try to be a flighty author, and for loving me unconditionally – even when I don't do the dishes!

Next I need to acknowledge Eric Lofholm who saw greatness in me from the first day we met and has spoken it into existence and changed my life through his advice, support and coaching.

I also have to send a shout-out to my wonderful friend Stacey Fabre who has, although we've just met, been such a great source for advice, support and belief that it's blown me away – you always give and give and give and I am eager to do the same for you!

I certainly couldn't have done this without the many, many people who supported me the moment they found out about this book through offers to review it, promote it, and encouraged me with their very kind words.

Last, I have to thank Alyssa Ann Evans (Soon to be Tubb) and Stephanie Lyda who, although we aren't as close as we once were, were the first people who ever believed in the power of my writing.

Foreword

"Whoever walks with the wise will become wise, but the companion of fools suffers harm." Proverbs 13:20

Friend Power. The principle of how your friends influence you cannot be underestimated.

As a mother of 7, business owner, and black belt in Taekwondo I know firsthand the power friends have on your life. I homeschooled Stephanie and her siblings because my husband and I wanted our children to be successful. We carefully chose the people we spent time with and who our children associated with. We knew that they were susceptible to the influences of their peers and adult mentors, so we worked to have positive people who supported our goals and belief systems in their lives. Often, parents called me. They wanted to know what to do to home school their own children. Why? Because they feared the negative influence of their child's peers at school. We want the very best for our children, so we try to surround them with people who will have a good influence on them. Why? Because we know Friend Power.

When our children entered college, I watched them and their childhood friends chose different paths as a result of their associations. Some abandoned their parent's faith because of the powerful influence of peers and professors. Straight A students almost lost scholarships because pull of peer acceptance lured these young adults into weekend parties. Why do serious college students form study groups to get better grades? Because they know the power of friends who spend weekends huddled at tables in the library, instead drinking at the local bars. One young ROTC cadet learned a sobering lesson when a commanding officer discovered he had been at a party with underage cadets drinking alcohol. That incident nearly cost him his Air Force commission.

As adults, though, we are sometimes blind to how we are influenced by the company we keep. My Taekwondo instructor invited me to test for my first black belt about 5 years ago. Eight of us worked together to earn the right to be awarded our black belts. Our instructors drove us to work together, coach each other and encourage each other. When someone was hurt, we supported them. If one failed, we all failed. If one succeeded, we all succeeded. We were invested in each other, and together we made it. If we want success, we need to surround ourselves with successful people.

What is your total success? What does that look like for you? Within the pages of this book, you will find insights about the company you keep. In the chapter, "The Everyman Mold", Stephanie illustrates the power of peer pressure to keep you right where you are. Never underestimate this power. To change the course of your life, you must be willing to take the steps necessary to break free from the Everyman Mold. To make sustainable change in your life, you must be willing to connect with the people who will support that change.

As Stephanie's mom and now business partner, I've seen this book come alive in her life. I watched her set goals and get involved with people who supported her achievement. Even when it meant raking wood shavings to muck out horse stalls for her mentors in the heat of Texas summers. When she decided to leave her corporate job to start her own business, she surrounded herself with coaches and friends who encouraged and equipped her to break from the Everyman Mold. The result of that is a successful young businesswoman and the book you are now reading.

This book will give you guiding principles to making lasting change in your life. Change can be scary. You need people to share your wins with, share their experience with you, and kick you in the pants when you're ready to give up. When I decided to take my business to a new level, I hired a coach who was doing what I wanted to do and I joined a powerful group of people who had trod the path I was embarking on. The following year I increased the revenues in my business by 50%. Does Friend Power work? You be the judge.

Are your ready for change? Are you ready to move in a different direction? Then read on. Stephanie practices what she preaches. You won't find fluff! She gives powerful evidence that you are a reflection of the people you surround yourself with. If you want change, be willing to look at the company you keep. Consider small steps to find the people who will support your dreams. Make friends with the wise. Step into a new life with *Friend Power*.

Anna Scheller, CCHP
Certified Sales Trainer and Coach
Co-host Black Belt Selling Radio Show
2nd degree Black Belt

Chapter 1
Introduction

Aesop's fables have great lessons for pretty much everyone on the planet who is willing and wanting to advance their life and those looking to improve their morals. In addition to the story above, one of the tales that always stuck out to me from the book of Aesop's fables my siblings and I passed around as children was the story of the farmer and the stork. In this particular story, a farmer spreads nets over his fields to catch the cranes and other mischievous birds that come to eat his seed and when he returns later that day, he finds a stork that has been hanging out with the cranes and wreaking havoc in the fields. The stork begs the farmer to spare his life – that he is nothing like the cranes, he is normally so much more cautious, careful, revered, etc. His arguments fail to change the farmer's mind and the farmer heartlessly tells the stork that if he chooses to hang out with the cranes and crows he will suffer the same fate as them.

Over and over again, while reading books such as *Think & Grow Rich* by Napoleon Hill and *The Millionaire Mindset* by T. Harv Ecker, it impresses me how they seem to agree with the farmer (though not necessarily in the same words). There isn't a single successful person that I've met that doesn't insist that to become successful yourself, you have to get yourself in the right mindset and you do so by reading, attending seminars, taking course, connecting with others of like mindset, etc.

Every time I read these books, my mind returns over and over to a moment that somehow ended up etched in my mind from my college days. Every English instructor I ever wrote for had the same request for me to submit my writings to the quarterly publication of student work. I particularly remember one instructor begging me to submit my work to be published and how it would help get me on my way to become a published author so I could share my gift with the world. I remember nodding, smiling and walking away from our consultation with scorn on my brow and in my mind: Why would I want to associate myself with these 'starving artists' who are all struggling to become someone and, from as far as I could tell, spend their group therapy sessions bashing on published authors who are less than worthy by the high standards of the group. I've seen those groups for years and they all suggest you get involved in one of their groups to become a published author. Start with a reading group, find a sharing group, work your way to the review board for a small publication of a collection of works and it will give you the practice needed to get anywhere in the real world.

My question always revolved around which member of their group "made it" according to the golden standard of fame they all aspire to by following their suggestions? Or, conversely, were they too busy embracing the starving artist image and collectively complaining over the success of those with less talent who just happened to know the right people. The next thought that always entered my head was "Seems easier to know the right people than to try and showcase your talent among a world of talented individuals." I was, and am, right! If you want to break out of the crowd and become successful, to borrow from Nike®, Just Do It!

There are literally millions of immensely talented people in the world. They are better singers, better actors, better dancers, better players than the select famous few. If talent and hard work is all it takes to be successful, what exactly is Kim Kardashian's claim to fame? What special talent does she offer that no other person in the world can do better? I'm not trying to pick on Kim here, you could put anyone in that sentence and ask the same question: what single talent makes that person irreplaceable or more deserving of his or her success than the next person?

My suggestion, as I will show multiple times in this book is to find a successful mentor, someone who has achieved what you are dreaming of achieving, and earn their respect and help. Miley Cyrus, Kim Kardashian, Stephanie Meyer, Justin Beiber, Christopher Paolini

– no matter what you have to say about their talent (or lack-there-of in some cases) or end product, everyone can admit that they got immensely famous in their respective times. I didn't pick those names for any reason other than I know that they have family and friend ties that brought them into the limelight and made their success substantially easier to accomplish. Clearly then, talent isn't everything!

So if talent isn't everything, what is? Aren't you tired of hearing "It's not what you know, it's who you know?" If you are, to be honest, you probably don't know the right people. And for a little more brutal honesty, it's probably your own fault. Before you get upset at me and throw the book down, ask yourself a couple of questions:

- Have I ever met anyone who has achieved the status I want?
- What have I done so I can meet someone who has achieved the success I am craving?

That's all you need to answer. If the answer to the first question is No, and the answer to the second question is something other than a laundry list of events you've attended, cities you've visited, emails you've sent, research you've done, or networking groups you're a part of, then you are cheating yourself.

There are stacks upon stacks of books about how to change your mindset to become wealthy and financially free and change your entire world. Very few of them touch on who you spend your time with. The extent of this coverage, as far as I can find, is limited to one chapter or a few paragraphs inside of a chapter. I have a stack of six books sitting on my nightstand right now that I'm working my way through, some of them for the second time, about the mindset of the financially free and successful and so far I haven't found a single one that puts the kind of emphasis on this single concept that I feel it warrants. I've noticed this idea pop up in articles over and over and once again, yet it gets no more than a cursory glance.

The trick is more than the mindset you choose for yourself. I believe that the company you choose to keep will have an inverse relationship on the mindset you develop about your life. No matter what good intentions you have for your mindset, unless you surround yourself with like-minded people, you will constantly struggle to maintain your positive change. If you choose to spend your time with those who are less successful and use their spare time to complain and gripe about how much their life sucks and how the world is out to get them, you will stay at the same level they occupy. I'm sure you've heard of the glass ceiling at work[1], I believe that there is one holding you back from your version of success too, and it is your friends and family. It takes an incredible person to break through the "glass ceiling" of their closest relationships and move above and beyond the level of talent and success that prevails in those circles.

Truthfully, when you move beyond the levels of success that your closest friends have accomplished, one of two things will happen: 1) You will move beyond that relationship into others or 2) they will grow with you. If they cannot grow with you, you don't need them in your life. I know that sounds harsh, but how long would you be able to enjoy hanging out with someone who is constantly complaining that they can't get over the same barrier you fought tooth and nail to conquer? Or someone who harbors jealousy or resentment at you, even under the surface, for what your hard work achieved? Take this piece of the book (and I will be bringing this idea up again, so don't think you're getting away from it) with whatever grain of salt you want or leave it on the table if you want. But in this instance, I am speaking from experience.

One final note before we get into the meat and potatoes of breaking what I call the Everyman Mold and evaluating the power of the friends you choose. This book isn't going to cover all the changes that need to happen in your mindset to achieve ultimate success. There are concepts such as how to change your mindset internally, setting goals, thinking bigger, adjusting your financial and mental

---

[1] For those of you who haven't, this is an unofficially acknowledged barrier to advancement in a profession, usually affecting women and members of minorities.

thermostat that are incredibly important to achieve success. These are all concepts that I won't be able to cover in detail within the borders of this book so if you are intent on changing your life, add this book to your library, but don't think that this book is a library in and over itself. I'm including a list of my favorite reading material at the end but I encourage you to find your own. There are hundreds of books out there that will change your life. Just as the Christian Bible is composed of 66 different books, create your own Bible of Success to guide you as you embark on the life-changing journey that is Finding Success!

Bon Voyage!

Chapter 2:
The Everyman Mold

In Earl Nightingale's audio book *The Strangest Secret*, he starts by telling you to take 100 young men at 25, all fresh and zesty with life, and imagine how many of them will be financially successful by the time they hit 65. He saves us the time of agonizing over the answer by informing us that only five out of 100 will "make the grade." The rest fall victim to, in my words, the Everyman Mold. In other words, life gets too hard, they are beaten into the same mold as every other man (or woman), and it's too difficult to pull themselves up by their bootstraps to realize their version of success, if they even know what that looks like to achieve it.

David J. Schwartz writes in *The Magic of Thinking Big*, "All around you is an environment that is trying to tug you, trying to pull you down second class Street. You are told almost daily that there are 'too many chiefs and not enough Indians.' In other words, [...] be content to be a little guy." Yet with every generation there are new opportunities to become one of the successful, affluent leaders that will head the pack for your generation. Think about it, as the old leaders retire, they leave a gap to be filled. The individuals who think everything has been done before, and there's no more room for wild success in the world except as actors and actresses are sadly mistaken. We will always live in a world of opportunity for those looking for it and those who take advantage of it will be richly rewarded.

Plainly speaking, the Everyman Mold is everything that holds you back. It is the idea that there are enough people changing the world so don't make waves or upset people. It is the notorious reminder to keep your opinions and plans to yourself. It is everyone who tells you that you are one in millions not one in a million, part of the crowd and not unique. It is everyone and everything that makes you feel that you are replaceable and the same as pretty much every other man or woman out there.

We are bombarded with these mindsets and thought patterns day in and day out. Supermodels on billboards have unattainable bodies, so we're told to not even bother trying. Be average, be normal, be happy. So many people are happy to explain that the Rockefellers, the Waltons and other blue bloods were at the right place at the right time and there's nothing else to do. The Everyman Mold is the thoughts that you're only one in hundreds in the art show, one of hundreds submitting books to the publisher, one of hundreds working for the company, so why should you expect to get ahead?

More damaging to your future and success than those thoughts are the sympathetic nods and pats on the shoulder that your friends give you: "Your art is so much better than his. But his dad is the janitor at the museum of art." "You work so much harder than Julie, you deserved the promotion. She only got it because she goes to happy hour with the boss every Friday." Those consolations are dangerous for many reasons. First, they are false reassurances that indicate that you aren't good enough to beat someone who has connections and while you're a great person, you'll never get ahead because the world is pitted against you. Second, they blatantly disdain those who use their connections to build the life they are dreaming of and find ultimate success. This consolation propones the idea that there are a thousand other talented, smart people out there just like you (true) but there's no reason you will be elevated above the others (false).

This is the Everyman Mold mentality. It is perpetuated by those who are struggling and believed by those who listen to them. To break out of that and find your ultimate success, you have to move beyond it. You have to determine your commitment to your success and if you want to ease and speed the path while nearly guaranteeing your future you must find the connections who can help you avoid the pitfalls that will slow you down. DON'T keep your head down. Put your chin up high. Believe in yourself and your value. Study those who have achieved success before you and mimic them. Spend time getting to know them and how they overcame their obstacles to achieve what you want. Most of all, know the pitfalls to avoid and let others guide you. The trick that I will be talking about in the rest of this book is that your friends will determine how focused you stay on breaking out of the Everyman Mold or how quickly you get sucked back into it.

This is incredibly important to realize because the information that you allow yourself to ingest day after day will feed your view of the world, your expectations, and your mindset on yourself. Have you ever heard of GIGO? Garbage in, garbage out. It was a phrase I learned as a kid to teach myself to control what I spent my time watching and listening to because that would manifest itself and come back out. The Bible has a very similar principle: "Out of the abundance of the heart, the mouth speaks" Luke 6:45b. In fact, the Bible spends a lot of time focusing on what you put into your mind. Any religion does because controlling the mind is the key to controlling your actions and your actions (in the religious example) determine how valuable of an addition you are to the religion. In your personal life, your mind determines your actions which will determine your level of success at what you want to do.

The important concept to understand here is that a huge portion of what you are exposed to every day is determined by the company you surround yourself with, the friends you choose for yourself, and the focus you place priority on. Consequently, what you expose yourself to every day will play a part in determining your future. If you allow yourself to be constantly barraged by the mentality that everyman is as good as you, you're no better than every other man/woman, you will fall prey to the Everyman Mold and live the same life that every other man/woman struggles through.

What would you prefer?

Chapter 3
What is Ultimate Success?

I use the phrase Ultimate Success very deliberately both here and throughout this book as opposed to the singular Success. During the course of your life you will experience many successes. Your ultimate success is the dream you harbor in your heart of hearts. You may get a promotion, buy a house, get married, have two kids and have the capability to go on a two week extravagant vacation every year and each of those may be a success in and of itself. However, the lifestyle you've created is the ultimate success I'm talking about finding through your friend power. You might get a painting purchased or a book published and while both of those are incredible successes to have, neither of them might be your dream of dreams and your ultimate success. Having a single painting purchased or featured in a museum or gallery doesn't make you the next Leonardo da Vinci or Pablo Picasso. Having a book published doesn't put you on par with JRR Tolkien or CS Lewis. When I discuss your ultimate success I am referencing the arrival at the ultimate success that each of your smaller successes are building.

That clarified, the first step I take with every coaching client is determining what they want. We spend an entire hour, and sometimes two working on just this one topic because, more often than not, we as humans get caught up in minutiae and lose track of where we are going and why we are going there. One of my favorite lines to use is that "the how-to isn't difficult, knowing what you want is the most difficult part of success." I encourage you to, as you read this book, think about what your ultimate success is because it is, at the end of the day, up to you. You are the only person who knows what the one thing you want so much that nothing will be able to get in between you and achieving that goal is. It's important to realize that whatever you plan for, you usually achieve.

This idea of achieving your plans works two ways! When you make plans to reach your version of success, you will usually accomplish that or some shadow of that. If you don't make plans and always have some vague shadowland you are heading towards, you will probably achieve that as well. The problem with heading into vague shadowlands is that it's kind of hard to tell when you arrive and if we learned anything from Disney's© *The Lion King* it's always a disappointment over what you thought it would be.

In this case, the answer to What is Ultimate Success? is going to vary based on what you want to accomplish and what you dream about. Too many people get caught up in the idea of success being a financial goal but success can be as simple as taking first place at the county show, replacing your income through online sales, or having your work featured at the Metropolitan Museum of Art.

Are you an artist looking to be the next Vincent Van Gogh? Are you looking to replace Madonna as the queen of pop? Do you want to make millions of dollars in passive income annually? Have you ever written that down and really thought about what that means? Saying that you want to be the best at something, or the most well-known, or the richest, or the most famous is an extremely vague definition and what I would refer to as the shadowlands. This isn't a goal setting book, if you need a reference to one check the My Reading Material at the end of the book, but this is an incredibly important concept and does warrant at least one short chapter.

Unless you have plans for what exactly your Ultimate Success looks like, you'll never know when you arrive, and you actually increase the likelihood that you will never arrive. Instead of being as famous as Madonna – why don't you try to sell more albums than she has, or perform more shows than she has to larger audiences. Instead of being one of the richest men on earth, make an intention to generate X amount of passive income every month, have a net worth of X amount and live in X neighborhood in a house valued at X amount and drive X car. Do you want to be the next famous designer or featured in certain magazines across the globe? Which of those is a measureable goal that you'll know when you achieve it?

Recently I spoke with someone who had the goal to put out a fashion magazine. When I told her that that was the easiest part of the goal she was confused. What she'd failed to define was how much of a reach she wanted with that magazine – whether she wanted it to be read across the globe or just in her local town? Whether she wanted to be the final word in fashion across the world or even just across the US was something that she had assumed she meant by stating that she wanted to have a fashion magazine. Unfortunately, by failing to truly define what she wanted, she made it all too easy to miss the true goal. Between the two of us, we could have had a fashion magazine up and running within a couple of months. Whether or not anyone who would read the magazine is a different story but by failing to define the parameters she intended, it would have been easy for her friends (and herself) to pat her on the back for just getting that far and not push to achieve what she had initially intended.

I hope this makes sense so when I talk about achieving your ultimate success, I am making reference to your personal definition of what success it. It doesn't have to be as great and incredible as some people, but it doesn't have to be limited by what you think you can actually accomplish either. Determine what you earnestly desire, how you'll measure it and what it means to you to accomplish that. Then find role models to follow who have already accomplished what you want to accomplish.

Before I end this chapter I do want to note that the power of your friends is not the only determining factor in achieving your ultimate success. It is a great way to ease the path, help ensure you will achieve your success and put you in position to live your dream, but it's not the only factor necessary. There will always be anomalies and I am sure that I will hear from plenty of individuals with stories about those who found success through the traditional routes or despite the company they were keeping. These variances are often enough to encourage all the other unhappy saps to keep following the traditional route instead of searching out new solutions. What I am presenting here is exactly that, a new solution to overcoming a world that is too full of talented individuals vying for the same success you are.

Chapter 4
Friend Power Defined

Hopefully this topic is fairly easy to understand and I'll be using most of the book to show you how to leverage your friend power, the amount of clout it holds and how to be aware of it in the pieces of your life you want to improve. In order to do that however, we need to have a common understanding of what friend power is and the influence it wields.

Friend Power has two pieces to it and both of them are just as important as the other.

First is the mindset that comes through the friends you keep. Think about it, imagine spending ten minutes, or even half an hour a day trying to change your mindset to achieve ultimate success and convince your self-conscious that it is possible. Then you spend the next two hours with a friend who is mostly interested in complaining about life or giving you the kind of false sympathy I outlined in chapter two. They are undoing everything you are trying to do. They are pouring negative thoughts back in and pulling you down – GIGO.

Eventually, you'll either have to tell them to stop complaining so much (and then hope that they actually listen to you) or move away from that poisonous relationship. Unfortunately, unless you have something better to replace that relationship with, you will either avoid nixing that relationship till it pulls you back down, or you'll move into a similar relationship with a new friend. That is the first piece of clout that is a part of this concept I call Friend Power.

The next important piece to understand is that your friends, more often than not, are the ones who provide you with advice on how to handle life. I remember a billboard I saw quite some time ago with an average looking woman on the ad and it said "Tax troubles?

Call (insert company name) first and your sister-in-law second." I thought this very nicely exemplified the second piece to Friend Power. While we all accept legal and medical advice from non-professionals in some cases, when the real value is on the line, we don't risk going to our friends and family. Isn't your success just as valuable to you? Why would you accept advice from someone who has never been in a position to implement it and gotten the results you're craving?

    I remember a long time ago my instructor in Sunday School was trying to make a point and brought in a gorgeous watermelon. He was getting us all excited about how he was going to cut into the watermelon and share it with us. He pointed out how vibrantly green the watermelon was, let us try and pick it up to see how heavy it was and got our mouths watering describing the sweet, watery goodness about to be in our hands. When he chopped the watermelon open everyone was shocked when black dirt poured out. My point in this story is that just because something (advice) sounds good, looks good and smells good, doesn't always make it good. It's your success, why leave it in the hands of someone who hasn't been in your shoes? Not that those people never have good advice, but if success was as easy as the advice that is handed out about it, more people would be enjoying their ultimate success right now.

    Robert Kiyosaki, the famous author of the *Rich Dad, Poor Dad* and real estate investment extraordinaire is an excellent example of how the company you keep can change the course of your future on both sides of the Friend Power sword. Very early in his life he began keeping company with his rich dad and that company changed his mindset and put knowledge of tools in his hand that elevated him well beyond anything he would have had the capability of dreaming of if he'd stayed inside his biological family's circles of friends. Not only did his rich dad teach him how to think about money and education, his rich dad also gave him tools to implement to grow his personal wealth.

    Just to be clear, I am not suggesting you go out and cultivate friends simply for the benefits they bring to your relationship. Friends for benefits is really more of a usury situation rather than actual friendship (which defeats the purpose of friend power). In addition to that, unless you actual enjoy spending time with these people, they probably won't enjoy spending time with you and you won't have the chance to develop the mindset you need to be developing. So while they might be able to give you the tools you need, your mindset will sabotage the implementation and the first hitch that comes up will be tallied up to the advisor not knowing what they were talking about.

What I am suggesting is that you be careful about who you allow to be your close friends. If you notice that the people you spend your time with fall into the molds I will be talking about throughout this book, and you have bigger goals and bigger plans, it might be time to start putting some distance between you two.

It's important to realize that a big part of the influence your friends have over you has to do with the story you are telling yourself. In essence this idea is that everyone alive is telling themselves a story about their lives and what they believe. Those stories shape how they view the world and how they respond to everything that happens to them. I first began to understand the power of the stories we tell ourselves while reading Seth Godin's book *All Marketers ~~Are Liars~~ Tell Stories*. The crazy part is that sometimes our stories don't correspond very well with everyone around us and that is often the stem for social differences. At the same time we all believe the stories we tell ourselves, otherwise we wouldn't tell ourselves them. In order to reassure our subconscious and validate our story, we search out other people who are telling themselves similar stories because it adds credibility to our story and makes us feel better about ourselves. This is why we often end up with friends who think and act just like we do and this is the trap that can keep Friend Power from elevating you.

Because of the power of your mindset over your action, the company you keep will either ensure you can never break the Everyman Mold, or they will break it for you. The friendships you choose will help determine your success in life and they certainly have the capacity to make your success easier beyond belief. Why would you choose to make your life harder than it needs to be?

Your friends, simply put, have the power to elevate you well beyond your current station in life, or keep you captive forever.

Chapter 5
Action Takers v. Action Talkers

I love this topic. Love it. I can't say enough about the power of taking action. I've talked for hours on this topic without getting tired. I've had people listen to me talk and afterwards tell me that they got tired just listening to me talk about taking action because I step out and act at such a high level. I've watched the world slip by those who would rather talk about how much they want things to change while I've actually stepped out and made the changes I wanted to see. I've also seen them jealously watch me walk away and heard the longing in their voices as they tried to convince me to come back.

In 2014 I started making huge changes in my life. I finally figured out what I wanted and within four months launched the business of my dreams enough to walk comfortably away from a full-time job. It required massive amounts of action and dedication on my part. When I started to make huge changes in my life, I found that I spent less and less time with those who liked to sit and talk about the changes they wanted to see and more time with other people who were taking the same amounts of massive action I was.

Those changes in the friends I chose were for two reasons. First, I stopped having time to sit and shoot the bull with those who could absorb a half hour or an hour of my time wishing for the world to change for them. Second, I found that when I spent time with the people who were taking the same amounts of action I was, I walked away invigorated and energized to get back to what I was working on rather than drained and pessimistic about the world around me.

If I'm completely honest, it's not always the action talker's fault. Action talkers are often bound by fear, complacency or laziness. While I don't have an excuse for complacency or laziness, I do understand the power that fear can have in paralyzing those who want to take action. Nearly a year before I was able to leave the company I was working for in 2014 things were so bad that I was started looking for a new job. After a half-hearted and very scared job search I gave up by telling myself that there are problems in every company and at least I know already I knew how to deal with the ones at my current company. Fear (and negative influences) are motivating the talkers and keeping them from taking action. Action talkers who find themselves in this situation have to use positive influences and surround themselves with action-taking friends if they ever hope to shift themselves from action talking to action taking.

It's not that the action talkers don't want results but there is something negative holding them back, often fear, and they don't have the people around them that they need to push themselves past the fear. There is always a concern, even with action takers, that the steps and changes they make will put them into a worse situation than before. The only way to get yourself past that paralyzing thought is to realize that you are never stuck where you end up and you can always change again. The key is to recognize this problem, this fear, and surround yourself with action takers who will help push you into taking action and encourage you past the dread of the unknown. Tony Robbins teaches that many times we will self-sabotage to some degree and we all have fear. Some of us fear failure, some of us fear success and all of that comes from wanting to be accepted and approved of by those that we love or care about. I feel that this is exactly why it's so important to surround yourself with action takers if you want to make a difference.

The truth is that sooner or later action takers will call action talkers on their BS and action talkers don't want to be called on that. They prefer to sit and talk about how wonderful the world will be when they finally arrive at the promised land. There's no risk in talking. These action talkers like planning and thinking about how to get there, but they don't want to expend the energy, or are too frightened of what could happen, to actually make these changes in their lives. Action takers don't have time for that. They make time to plan but it's only a small portion of their day. Action takers are absorbed with results and getting results and they stay up till 1am and get out of bed again by 6am in order to see their dreams come true. Action takers know that they can't afford to spend 60% of their day dreaming about how wonderful the future will be because they are too busy building it and loving every minute.

Action takers also look for paths to achieve what they are talking about, action talkers only look at how magnificent it will be to get there. While action talkers might make plans on how to arrive, they never figure out how to take the next step or actually take that step. For the action talkers, it's more fun to plan and dream than it is to actually work and sweat to arrive. Action takers know to break things down into manageable steps and not, to borrow a terrible cliché, count eggs before they are hatched. The action talkers have rarely, if ever, had the opportunity to taste the fruits of success, and the action takers are so addicted to the taste of success that they are constantly finding new ways to get their hands on it.

One of the biggest dividers between the action takers and the action talkers is that the action takers get results. These are the ones who achieve success over and over again and this breeds both resentment and jealousy in the action talker. The action talker will often begin to feel inadequate compared to the action taker because the action taker is actually achieving so much. The talker sees the years go by with hardly any difference year over year. Because of this, action talkers don't seek out action takers to spend time with – I don't know a single person in the world who likes feeling inadequate or jealous. Any relationship that regularly makes you feel like either of those emotions is one you'll begin to avoid.

Last but not least, action takers are, quite simply, too busy taking action to spend time sitting with the action talkers about all the plans they have for the future. Action talkers spend most of their day talking and action takers spend most of their day doing. The talkers make the highlight of their day in the talking and the takers use talking only to motivate themselves to higher results and hold themselves accountable. While an action taker might spend time with an action talker for a while in hopes of motivating the talker into taking action to improve his or her life, if the talker won't start taking action, the taker will begin to move away rather than risk falling back into inaction.

Taking action is the only way to be successful at any of the elements I've outlined in this book. Unless you apply the information you're learning here, the time you spent reading this and the time I spent writing this hasn't done you a bit of good. Whenever I speak live I like to encourage my audiences not to waste the time they've spent with me and I want to do the same right now. Make today your, as my mentor calls it, line-in-the-sand day. The day you're not going back from. The day you are making a change in your life and becoming an action taker.

Chapter 6
Friends Pave Your Career

There are so many ways that the power of your friends determines your career in a traditional job that it is almost terrifying. In fact, this is probably the chapter that most people thought of immediately when they found this book. If I'm honest, this is one for the first chapters I started to flesh out when I started writing this book. Friend power can determine everything from the interview through promotions, and even termination in some cases!

Haven't we all been told at some point in our lives that someone can get an interview for us? It's a classic line in any TV show where the frustrated parent arranges an interview for his or her kid to go get a job so the child can become a productive member of society. The scene that usually follows is the parent shoving the child into a suitable pair of clothes and out the door – occasionally it even ends with the parent driving the child to the interview itself. The results of the interview always vary depending on which route the TV show wants to take, however my point is in the interview itself. When I applied for my first job, it took me multiple emails and calls to get my first interview, and multiple emails and calls to get my second interview. While I'd nailed both interviews, and I was later told that the manager had intended to hire me but was busy and it fell behind on his agenda (so another manager hired me into his department instead), it was a lot of work just to get the interviews!

Imagine instead of a friend or family member had happened to know Mr. Flores and asked him to give me an interview. I'm sure I could have been in the office within a few days instead of after weeks and weeks of pestering. At that time, I spent hours around my family members and professors who were giving me advice on what to do. I looked up information online and was ready for those interviews. If I'd, instead, surrounding myself with friends who had never gotten a job, much less passed an interview, I would have never placed the needed priority on it to get the job. In this case, my friend power gave me the knowledge, mindset and tools necessary to ace the interviews.

The power of the friends you surround yourself with is substantially further than just getting or acing an interview. Have you ever noticed how upper management tends to spend most of their time together? Between meetings, lunch, happy hour, smoke breaks and office parties, there is a theme. Management hangs out with management. Taking things a step further, have you ever noticed how, when someone on the floor starts to get along with the upper management and joins them at every opportunity possible, a promotion tends to right around the corner? Before you shrug this off as giving favors to friends, let's examine this idea a little bit more.

While there certainly is a tendency to promote friends to managerial positions, there are also enough rules in place (usually) to prevent this from being the only reason the person gets promoted. While it does help the managers to know that whoever they invite into their circle will be a good fit, there's a lot more at stake. While the constant engagement does tend to keep the regular Joe at the forefront of management's mind when a position does become available, there's also something to be said about the constant exposure that is available and the learning opportunities that were available over and over again throughout that engagement.

I knew a man who had devoted more than 20 years of his life to the United States Air Force and, despite repeat recognition for excellence in work, he was passed over in his attempts to reach the rank he wanted. I'd known this man for quite some time when all this happened and didn't understand how that could happen. I didn't know anyone else more dedicated to the mission than he was (except perhaps my own father!). In addition to that as far as I was aware, he was always well-loved by his immediate supervisors. It took me a long time to puzzle through my memories and understand why he wasn't rewarded for his hard work and expertise by recognition with a promotion. It wasn't until recently that I realized that it had nothing to do with his skills.

The friends that this man surrounded himself with at that time taught him that spending his time rubbing elbows on the golf green or hanging out with co-workers at the Club after work was brown-nosing – an extremely negative connotation no matter how you look at it. Those friends reinforced his belief that networking was a waste of time for hard working officers and those who spent their time clinking glasses and hitting balls instead of improving the mission were spineless suck-ups and a waste of military space.

I finally understand that not receiving a promotion to the next rank, or promotion in any industry, has little to do with the quality of performance that a worker shows and more about the influences in their life. While there were many more factors at play in this situation than solely the friends my acquaintance kept, the people he spent his time with didn't value making those much-needed connections. Endorsements are vital for rank progression in any professional organization and when your friends view that kind of networking as a negative influence on your life, they will pull you away from the very connections you need to grow your career.

For this family friend, his workplace friends validated his view that spending his leisure time with higher-ranking officers instead of his family put work ahead of family and compromised his belief system. The criticism of his peers was like crabs in a trap. When a crab in a trap tries to climb out and escape, the others in the group will pull it back down. Any attempts by my friend to change his circumstances and surroundings would have resulted, even if it was subconscious on their parts, in his friends pulling him back into the trap.

It's the same in nearly every industry out there. Promotions are less about the quality of performance that the worker shows and more about the upper management's confidence in the worker's ability to handle the stresses of a management position. The truth is, and I know several leadership and management trainers who will agree with me, that the ability to do your job has very little to do with your capability to manage a team. A great worker won't always make a great manager and in corporate American (and in the USAF) it's not easy to un-do a promotion if it turns out that the promoted individual isn't able to handle it. Precisely because of that fact, it's more reliable to promote someone you know who does a moderate or great job at their position but you know has the skills and characteristics necessary to become a great manager rather than someone who performs exceptionally but may not be mentally ready to handle a team.

Just like in our other cases, there are two sides to the power of your friends. I recently saw an article online by Jeff Haden, Inc. Magazine contributing editor, about how the way you look and dress affects your career. In the article he takes us back to his early days working at a factory. He indicates that he was generally well-liked and got along great at least with his co-workers. One day his boss came and took him aside and asked him where he wanted to go with the company. Ever the aspiring young worker, Jeff told the boss that, eventually, he'd like to take over the boss's position. The boss was, surprisingly, extremely encouraging and stated that that was a real possibility. He then gave the young Mr. Haden a phenomenal piece of advice: How could he expect to run the company when he was acting and dressing like a regular worker? The young man gave the same response that anyone would expect: that he shouldn't be judged on his appearance, solely on the quality of his work. Unfortunately, the boss responded, that's not how the world works. Can you imagine how frustrated Jeff would have been to spend his entire life wondering why his excellent work wasn't enough to get past his long hair and ripped jeans?

The power your friends have over your success reaches much further in career than just corporate jobs. Entrepreneurs are probably one of fastest growing industries in the world. New businesses are launched every day. New ideas are created, patented and thrown into the world. But 95% of those businesses won't make it to the ten year mark or to the incredible success that the final 5% others will enjoy. The ones that become great are the ones that surround themselves with other leaders who can guide them through the pitfalls of starting a business and keep the entrepreneur's mind open to more greatness than he or she can see in the immediate toil through the trenches of building a business from scratch.

The knowledge that the company you surround yourself is aware of and can share with you can completely change your future. When you surround yourself with people who have the knowledge and the capability to change your future, and work hard to not only be friends with them, but impress them, they will return the favor through golden nuggets and right connections at the right times.

Beyond even promotions, interviews and building a business, it is incredible how your friends often become your mentors. I was recently advised that it is a highly encouraged piece of Microsoft's corporate culture for every employee to have a mentor within the company. The person who brought this to my attention also mentioned that these mentors regularly become your friends, or that employees choose their friends to be their mentors. It's a perfect example of how friend power is making its magic in the workplace. Your mentors advise you on what to do, how to act, how to interact, how to do your job and more. That advice often determines where your career ends up and, once again, it comes down to who you surround yourself with and the friends you choose.

Again, all of this isn't trying to say that you'll never make it to upper management without heeding this information, but the path to success is certainly shaped at least in part by the people you encounter and the friends you choose. Once again, there's logic behind the old adage: it's not what you know, it's who you know. There are solid reasons that this mentality carries over to the workforce. Next time, before it becomes a pout-fest that you were passed over for the promotion because Jaden is friends with the boss, remind yourself that there are reasons that promoting Jaden was a safer move for the company and, if you are determined to move along in your company, invest time with your managers, or their managers.

Chapter 7
Becoming Financially Free

I will be the first to admit that this was a fun chapter to add to this book! Financial success (however you define that) is probably one of the most sought-after goals in most of the world. I would venture to say that it is one of the most highly written about topics in the non-fiction world and there are literally millions upon millions of dollars generated from seminars, courses and literature about creating financial success every year. So why aren't more people financially successful?

My opinion is that it comes down to one main reason: these attendees have not surrounded themselves with the people necessary to support their goal. These seminars spend entire weekends teaching the proper mindset and the right kinds of tools to become financially successful. Any seminar that is doing its job sends the attendees home pumped beyond belief, and many of them even walk attendees through the first few stages of applying the tools they teach. The problem is that these attendees may spend a total of 20 hours at these seminars trying to change a mindset that has been ingrained through a lifetime of experience. They top that off by going back to their old lives and their old friends who may or may not be supportive, but who probably haven't achieved financial freedom and success or know what it takes to make that happen.

When I originally wrote the first sentence in that prior paragraph, I originally stated that there were two reasons for this lack of follow-through but the more I thought about it, the more I realized that the second reason was a symptom of the first! Originally I stated that the second reason so many people fail at this objective is because it simply becomes too hard however I realized afterwards that it's only too hard when it's no longer forefront in their mind. When something is consuming your thought process, nothing is too difficult to overcome to achieve that goal.

    First of all, I need my readers to realize that there are multiple levels of financial success. What may look like success to one person may not be success to another. One individual may be looking for millions of dollars in passive income annually, another may only want five figures of passive income (passive income, by the way, is income that you don't have to do anything to achieve because when your money is working to create more money). Another individual may be looking to become debt free or manage their finances and be able to pay their bills and live comfortably on their income and if they achieve this, they will have achieved their version of financial success.

    For the individual who wants to start building passive income to replace working income, it's imperative that they are constantly surrounded by wealthy, financially-free individuals. The entrepreneur that takes this step is many times more likely to take advantage of the wealth of knowledge that is available through their friends and apply it over and over again until their personal wealth accumulates to the same levels as their comrades. Those individuals that end up feeling that financial freedom through passive income is too big of a goal and too hard to attain are not receiving the proper support from their closest associates.

    Again, it comes down to the two sides of your friend power: the knowledge they offer and the mindsets they encourage. Financially affluent friends often know the tools to become financially affluent and they don't mind sharing that information with those close to them. They often already know much of what the seminars will teach because they've attended (or written) them, read the books, surrounded themselves with the appropriate people and applied the tools ceaselessly until they achieved success. They know how to hold you accountable and push you through the pain without any of the false and dangerous sympathy that gives you an option of sinking back into mediocrity.

In the very beginning of this book I touched on Robert Kiyosaki's story. If your goal is financial freedom, I highly recommend you become intimately familiar with his story. Find your "rich dad." Not Sugar Daddy. Rich Dad. Your rich dad doesn't even have to be a man. But it should be someone who will walk you through the mindset, hold you accountable to keep that mindset in place, help you get your feet firmly planted and, if nothing else, be able to point you in the right directions to get the tools you need to find your success. Lastly, your Rich Dad will hold you accountable to achieve the success you desire.

On the other side of financial success, if your goal is to pull yourself out of debt, do you think that's going to be possible with a group of friends who are constantly charging things to cards, taking out bigger mortgages to sustain bigger houses and more expensive car loans? There is hot debate over the concern about how easy it is to buy now and pay later. I've read many books where the author discusses the problem that most middle-class families face. The problem is that they are so connected to keeping up with the Smiths that they don't have a problem taking out a second mortgage or opening a new credit card in order to save face and keep appearances up. There's a stigma for those who haven't achieved the American dream of a car, a family, a house and a well-paying job. Too many jobs don't pay well enough for a car, a house and a family, so they go deeper and deeper in to debt to live the American dream. Then the smart ones get life insurance to pay off their debts when they die so those debts don't get passed on to the family to shoulder.

As long as you surround yourself with the people that find it easier to charge it than earn it, you'll always struggle to get out of debt and keep up with them like we all inherently want to do. It helps to realize that these people can rarely afford what they are purchasing for themselves either, but it hardly matters when the friends you choose would prefer to leverage debt to live the lifestyle they desire than restrain themselves and live well down the road. Dave Ramsey and his following are excellent groups of people to surround yourself with if this is your ultimate financial success. They have the mindsets, they have the tools, and rather than scorning you for holding off on a vacation or big purchase until you can afford it, they will support you and encourage you.

Again, it comes down to knowing what you want, and finding other people who have either achieved your goal or are working towards your goal to spend your time with to keep yourself focused, keep it forefront in your mind, and keep yourself accountable.

Chapter 8
Friends & Fitness

Once again I'd like you to think back, this time to the last time you saw a fitness fanatic hanging out with a couch potato. It doesn't really happen. These two individuals hang out in different locations, absorb themselves in different activities, and lead pretty different lives. Even those who are mildly fit don't tend to spend their time around those who are extremely out of shape and those who are extremely fit don't tend to spend their time around those who are even mildly fit. I've watched the interactions at my local gym over the past 12 months and I've watched some individuals who started hanging out with my personal trainer regularly and now I hardly recognize them they have buffed up so much.

Once again this proves my point that the company you choose will either bring you up or pull you down until you reach their level. In this case, since these individuals hung out at the gym with my trainer, they were pulled up to his level. Another great example is a very close family member of mine. She began, a quite few years back, to date an avid skier. Prior to beginning a relationship with that individual she had always been careful about her health and worked out at an average pace on a regular basis and had only skied once in her life. While she was in excellent shape and certainly in better condition than most individuals her age, she wasn't necessarily an athlete in the competitive sense of the word. The man she began to date was an exceptional athlete in a very demanding sport (cross-country skiing) and not only competed regularly but won regularly as well.

Under his influence, this family member became an endurance athlete and cross-country skiing became such a permanent part of her life that she continued the sport even after she moved on from that relationship. Now she trains intently year-round to meet the demands of her sport and improve her results. Her vacations are, most of the time, skiing vacations and her fitness regimes are designed to provide her with better ski times. At an age when most of her peers are declining in physical prowess and leaving the competition to the younger crowd she is still stronger, fitter and faster than most women half her age.

For those who are struggling to lose weight, it often has to do with the company they surround themselves with as much as it has to do with themselves. If you want to get fit and lose weight, spend time around fit, healthy, active individuals. Rather than spending every evening around the bbq with a beer in hand, they are on the bike trails or hiking trails. They are at the gym or a yoga studio. They are conscious about what they eat and how it affects their body. The more time you spend with these individuals, the more time you spend conscious of your food choices and active.

It's a little bit of a chicken and egg perspective though. In order to change your fitness level, you need to start seeking out and finding those who perform at the levels you want to perform at and spend time with them to develop friendships. But it would be extremely difficult for a couch potato to go start spending time with a personal trainer and become close friends. Like with most of the other areas of your life that your friend power influences, if you don't enjoy spending time around those people, as soon as they start challenging you to change your perspective (or if you're trying to get more fit, your body will start to ache and hurt and cry for you to stop), it will be easy to stop. The more you enjoy hanging out with them, the more likely you are to push through the pain to do it anyhow.

This is the concept behind fitness clubs and health clubs and Weight Watchers®. The idea that when you're surrounded by people with a similar goal and a similar mindset, you'll attain similar results. That is probably the best description of friend power in this entire book.

Chapter 9
The Key to Spirituality

The two most hotly contested and debated topics on the face of the earth are politics and religion. Want to start a debate on social media? Voice your opinion about the current governing body, world relations, gun control, abortion, gay marriage, or religion. This is such an important concept for most people that they cannot develop close friends who do not support their religious worldview. While some more open-minded individuals may try to keep this concept from influencing their decision in friends and in developing relationships, it still makes it difficult more often than naught to become close friends with someone who supports a different worldview than you do.

Let's take that a step further. How involved with your religion do you want to be? Many times the people that you spend your time with will have the same level of commitment that you do. Part of this is because if you are always at (in this example) church, you are likely to become close friends with the others who are always at church. If you are a weekend-only attendee, you tend to become close with other weekend-only attendees. These attendees may not even attend your church, but because they share roughly the same religious views as you do, it's easy to become closer to those individuals. Because those individuals also find it acceptable to only attend on the weekends or holidays, it adds credibility to the story you tell yourself that your attendance on weekends and holidays are the right way to do it.

Again, because of how personal and heated this topic gets, I want to add a disclaimer that neither of these mindsets are necessarily right. I'm not looking to judge you for the mindsets you have or indicate that one is better than the other. I'm just trying to state the facts that I've observed over my life and particularly over the past two years. Individuals who are extremely engaged in their religious activities spend their time around others who support that action and those who have other interests in their life spend their time with others who share those interests instead.

More than just religious and strictly in the sense of a church (because I believe that your spirituality is not determined by the church you attend or how often you attend it), but how you view the world morally will influence who you spend your time with. If you don't believe that a certain action is acceptable, let's use intolerance for human rights abuse for this example, you are not likely to spend your time around a slave trader, or even a member of the Westboro Baptist Church because their particular viewpoint does not mesh with yours. If you strongly feel that everyone is entitled to their own opinion and it doesn't need to reflect yours in order to be right in their eyes, you won't spend your time around someone who is intolerant of anyone else who disagrees – even if you agree on fundamentally every other religious and spiritual concept.

Most of the examples I've used show how you choose your friends based on your beliefs, however since this book is about the power that your friends have over you, I'd like to take another turn here. Let's go back to the first example of someone who has been a weekend-only church attendee. In this example let's pretend that this person or family decides to change churches (whether because of a move or because they feel so led, it doesn't matter the reason in this case). At this new church, they begin to make new friends and the new friends are extremely involved in the church, extremely dedicated to the vision of the church and unbelievably zealous for their church family and deity. This new family or couple or handful of individuals that will be making friends with our example couple spend at least three nights a week at the church for various activities or with church members. Because our example individual likes spending time with the members of the new church, they start to accept invitations to attend more and more church related events. As our sample group spends more and more time at these church-related events, they receive more and more exposure to the beliefs that drive their friends. They have more conversations and develop their own set of beliefs that reflect the story they have been told over and over again inside these church events.

The vice versa is true as well. If you take a strong-believer, someone who, previously, had spent 3+ nights a week with church family and begin to fill their life with other, weekend-only or non-religious individuals, the religion will get put on a back burner. It's no mistake that churches offer so many opportunities to get involved with the members, because they understand the power of your friends over your life. The Christian Bible talks repeatedly about staying engaged with the congregation and not allowing yourself to fall out by yourself. I like to think that this is because God already knows the power that your friends have over your decisions and understands that this theory holds power.

If our sample individuals in the first example continue to spend their time with those church-minded groups, they will eventually develop the same beliefs and the same mindsets that drive their friends. It's impossible not to. Napoleon Hill mentions the concept of autosuggestion in his book *Think And Grow Rich* and the idea of autosuggestion is that whatever you tell yourself often enough and over enough, you'll eventually believe. There are power in words and the words you hear from your friends will influence your beliefs whether you expect it to or not.

Chapter 10
Family Life & Friend Power

I've been a little reluctant to include this chapter. For the same reasons I don't want my readers going out and trying to find and use/abuse friends to get their connections and help, I don't want anyone to think that I'm condoning some of the examples I'll use to try and get exactly what they want out of life. This is an extremely hot topic for many people and just as much as in other chapters, friend power isn't the only key to success, it's just one aspect of finding success in this arena.

This chapter also ties pretty heavily in with chapter 12 as your family will often determine your emotional health levels, but there were enough differences that I felt they warranted two separate chapters.

First things first, have you ever noticed that single people, normally, hang out with single people or young married couples and married couples[2] sometimes intermingle with single people but more often spend time with other young couples and parents rarely intermingle with singles? There are all sorts of reasons behind this concept, but again part of it comes down to supporting the story you are telling yourself as I discussed previously. Your story is your entire life and you see the world through your lens. Single people look through one set of lenses and married couples look through a slightly different set and parents look through an even further removed set of lenses. Parents see the world as it can affect their children, singles see

---

[2] In this case I am using the term married couple to refer to anyone who is inside of a long-term and dedicated relationship with one other person.

the world as it can affect them and married couples see the world as it affects them and their partner.

The long and short of it, again, is that what you want to become, you usually need to surround yourself with. As soon as a single person starts spending all their time around married couples, sooner or later a significant other is often in the works for the single individual. Once a married couple starts to spend time around a couple with children, children tend to follow shortly as well for the (previously) household of two. I'm not necessarily saying that you need to force yourself to spend all your time with the group of individuals you want to become, but again I am suggesting you to be aware of the power it has over your future.

Just as important as knowing that these relationships have power of your future, it's important to know why. In the case of single individuals, it's a mindset about whatever their thoughts are on marriage. One group of singles tends to disdain it vigorously, the other tends to be so desperate to find true-love that they are jumping into relationships left and right. Neither of these mindset is right, wrong or all-inclusive. But they both exist and both have influence over your future. If everyone in your group of friends is jumping into relationships, it's easy to settle for whoever you find that might possibly be a good match. If all of your friends scorn relationships, it's just as easy to have invisible guards over your heart to avoid breaking the camaraderie of the relationship. Being aware of this can make it possible for you to craft your own future based on your own desires.

Likewise, both singles and young married couples tend to look at parents one of two ways: with longing to create that happiness in their own life, or derision over the struggles of parenthood and the parents who are clearly unprepared or too immature to be bringing that into their lives or the world. I'll keep repeating it, but neither of these mindsets is all-inclusive or the "right" mindset to have. They just are what they are. Just like with the singles, most couples will strive to maintain the constancy of their relationships with their friends and so if it's acceptable among their friend circles (and they have the inclination themselves), they will lean towards starting a family. If it's a hot subject of ridicule and frequent scorn among friends, it's not likely that the couple, no matter how much they do or don't want it, will create a family as long as those relationships exist.

If you're still not convinced, you might be part of the minority that blurs these lines a bit, but more often than not, the blurred lines don't lead to the kinds of deep and fulfilling relationships that can be found among similar familial-minded groups. There's often either a lack of relationships, a parting of ways, or a lack of truly deep relationships among those that move into these separate groups.

Chapter 11
Stunt or Support Your Personal Growth

Next to finances, personal growth is probably the second most written-about topic and offered seminar in the non-fiction world. It might even give financial wealth a run for its money if I'm totally honest. No matter how you intend to grow, if you surround yourself with friends, that growth becomes exponentially easier or absolutely non-existent.

Let's take a pretty classic example of college which is a great form of personal growth. College students probably spend more time each week growing and learning than many full-time adults. They attend lectures, read books, write papers and then get tested to determine how much they actually retained. This is also an incredible example of how the company you keep can determine how much growth you'll have. Students who attend the same school, take the same classes and graduate with the same degree have, usually, the same amount of personal growth possible. Why will some students explode with growth and others come out no more mature and level-headed and ready to add value to the world than a high-schooler?

This is probably the most obvious example in this book. One student spent his or her time surrounded by intellectual students and the other probably spent the majority of his or her time living the classic college party life. In this case, both had the same opportunities but the friends they chose completely change the future they will have. What is interesting is that the student who chose to grow and take advantage of the opportunities he or she had in college will likely continue that habit of self-growth throughout the rest of his or her life – with or without the help of friends surrounding him or her. As I'll show later, this is likely, but not guaranteed.

Beyond the hallowed halls of school, there is something to be said for the adult who spends weekends at seminars to grow their personal mindsets and world-views, who purchases books to read them to expand how they look at the world. These are the adults who, usually, make it a priority to travel and meet new friends around the globe. These are the adults who look at the world through a difference lens and realize that there are a variety of viewpoints out there, none of them are wrong per-se and not all of them are bad. However, and again I am speaking from personal experience, these habits tend to fall by the way-side without someone in your life to support them.

If everyone you surround yourself with is happy with the mindsets they currently have and don't feel a need to expand their mindsets and grow their perspectives, you are not likely to feel that way either. Once again it comes down to the stories that we tell ourselves. If the people you surround yourself with are constantly indicating, through their own quest for personal growth (mentally and skillfully) that there is always room to grow and always focus on increasing, you are more likely to pursue the same results. You'll take opportunities to attend seminars that might otherwise have been skipped over. You'll pick up books that otherwise might not have interested you. You'll find yourself growing your mindset and your skillset without much thought about that exact process.

On the other hand, when I found myself at a job where everyone I spent time with felt that they were sufficiently versed in the world, I was very resistant to continuing my own growth – even though I was the student in college who was spending all my time with the honors crowds. I was so resistant and so overly confident in my own knowledge that when I was presented with an opportunity to take a course for free, I snubbed that opportunity for a whole year. I picked up books, occasionally, but overall was comfortable with the idea that I was in a good place mentally and after four years of rigorous study, I didn't need to put such emphasis on it anymore.

Obviously I've had some attitude adjustments since then. I was introduced to an incredible set of people who helped me see that there was substantially more to learn than I knew – even on topics I thought I was already well versed in. That was the jump-start that I needed to begin building my personal growth library and efforts once again. Because of my past experience with studies, it certainly made it easier to get back into the habit, however the people I surrounded myself with for a year made it difficult to continue naturally.

The power in personal growth is two-fold. A very wise person once said "If you're not growing, you're dying." Which should be incentive enough for anyone to look at personal growth as a must-have for your life. I don't know many people who want to be dying or who want to go through life slowly dying inside. Which leads to the next benefit of making personal growth a priority: if you want to make changes in your life, which I am assuming by picking up this book you are looking to make changes in your life, you will have to grow to reach new levels. Just like it's impossible to reach the top shelf without growing or climbing on some sort of height-enhancing tool (counters and stools count!), you'll never reach new heights in your own life unless you grow to accommodate them.

Choose friends that will encourage personal growth in order to make it a priority in your life.

Chapter 12
Emotional Handling: Healthy or Hurting

This chapter is such a big deal to me because I've seen so many people struggle to even realize that some of the ways they handle emotions are unhealthy much less make an actual change in how they handle those emotions. This is such a big deal to our society that there is an entire professional class dedicated to helping you handle your emotions: psychologists. There are books upon books about handling your emotions and living a healthy life that is not overwhelmed by an unnatural balance. There are coaches who make their entire living off helping people develop emotional buoyancy and resilience and psychotherapists were, at one time, arguably one of the highest paid professionals in the country.

The problem is that it doesn't matter how many books you read about taking care of yourself, controlling your emotions, being assertive and getting past your fears. You must remove yourself from the relationships that are encouraging and creating these feelings in yourself, or place yourself in relationships that will stand up to you and hold you accountable to a higher standard you'll struggle for the rest of your life to grow emotionally.

This is a difficult chapter to write because, once again, I don't want to insinuate anything and particularly not that people who struggle with emotional imbalance are emotionally crippled and beyond help or that your friends are the only determining factor here. It's a fight to overcome whatever emotional state you have grown up with and move on to find a better place to exist. It requires energy, focus, determination, and support. If any of those pieces are missing, it's nearly impossible to overcome whatever is holding your emotional health back.

Because emotions impact how you react to and view the world, your emotional health has a very strong effect on the results you will live and it's extremely important for us to be on the same page regarding what I mean by emotional health. For me, an emotionally healthy individual is one who understands balance in emotions and isn't driven to extremes one way or another. This is a person who realizes that there is value in human life and that they have value to add to the world.

For me, an emotionally healthy individual is one who doesn't rely on anyone else in the world to determine who he or she is and how one views one's self and the life he or she will live. Emotionally healthy people don't rely on the views of others to determine their own self-worth. Emotionally healthy people don't have to stay in relationships because of some kind of affirmation they receive through the relationship. Emotionally healthy people don't live a life full of regrets and hatred. Emotionally healthy people don't build themselves up at the expense of anyone else. While this definition still feels somewhat simplistic, it gives a better idea of what I'm trying to convey with this chapter.

Despite that definition, even the most balanced and emotionally strong person in the world will still be prone to determine his worth in part by the way the world views him. There is a strong element in how you view your worth that is determined by the people you spend your time with. If they are constantly building you up and both telling you and exhibiting belief in your abilities, you will eventually begin to feel much the same way. It's a little bit of the celebrity mindset – after so many people tell a celebrity that they are incredible and wonderful and all-that, it's hard to remain humble and stay true to your roots. You don't have to take it quite that far, but think about the last celebrity that went a-wall on paparazzi or some innocent bystander for not recognizing who they were. Somehow, I highly doubt that person intended to go crazy over the fame, but the more often you hear support, the more likely you are to believe it.

Conversely I'd like to, with great caution since I understand that there is a lot more coming into play in this situation than just the power of friends, take an extreme situation of an abusive relationship. In most abusive relationships, the abuser keeps the victim inside the relationship by blaming the victim for the abuse and barraging the victim with the belief that this is normal and acceptable and the victim has little to no worth to the world. That constant exposure to those beliefs by a partner make it extremely difficult to pull back far enough to realize that that kind of mentality isn't healthy and isn't normal.

A lot of the concern I have with healthy handling of emotions comes back to your friends holding you back to levels of emotional instability through the same false sympathy I warned is so dangerous earlier. The wrong friends will often, rather than helping you pull yourself out of your struggles and help you find a way through them, try to empathize with you and give you the belief that your struggles are normal and it is okay without helping you get past them. My suggestion is to realize that while they may be normal to some extent, if you're not happy, it's not okay.

I am not necessarily claiming that all emotional health problems can be overcome through the company you surround yourself with. There are a lot of factors that come into play with emotional health. However, I do believe that the friends you choose either make it easier to grow emotionally and live a stable, healthy life through examples and advice or hold you into whatever rut you've struggled with up till now.

Chapter 13
Starving Artists Want to Be Starving Artists

The problem I have with most starving artists is that they are following a broken system – otherwise they wouldn't be starving (emphasis on Starving) artists! It's not often that you hear of someone making it from the position of wannabe to world-famous because of their support group which meets in the library basement every Wednesday or on the First Friday Art Walk every month. I've already mentioned that I have a slight problem with these groups because the ones I've participated in are usually full of griping over those who have made it to the realm of the successful or the false sympathies I covered earlier.

I actually have a much bigger concern than just the waste of time I've spent on those groups. First off is that many of these starving artists fall prey to the victim mentality which, as I'll discuss in chapter sixteen, cripples your shot at success. Next, like I mentioned in the beginning of this chapter, it's a broken system. Many of them survive under the belief that if they put their hours in and get good enough, eventually they will get There. Not surprisingly enough, There is usually some vague, ambiguous definition of success that may or may not be as great as J.R.R. Tolkien, Julie Andrews or Vincent Van Gogh. Outside of sending off hundreds of manuscripts and expecting them to come back refused, or participating in every First Friday Art Walk, or going out for hundreds of auditions, what other advice do these peers usually have to offer you? Have any of them ever made it that greatness you desire? In all likelihood, they have not. But for some reason, everyone who wants to become famous in the arts industries seems to think that being part of a starving artist group is the key to success. I'm here to tell you otherwise.

Those people are so busy being starving artists that they have no time to plan their goals and look at all the possible routes to achieve success. They are less than qualified to give you advice on how to do anything but exactly what they are doing. They spend all their energy following a path that might have worked forty or fifty years ago, but there was much less competition back then. There wasn't such an art to achieving your ultimate success as there is now.

In the chapter on the victim mentality I will talk about the dangers of romanticizing that mentality and there is just as much danger here. Most artistic wannabes start out by romanticizing and idealizing the starving artist image. It's generally understood, in those groups, that they will have to make it through the starving artist phase before they will make it big and the best way to make it through is to surround yourself with other starving artists who will be able to encourage you and uphold you as you go through it. Eventually, these extremely talented and artistic individuals give up their dreams and chain themselves to a desk just to make ends meet so they can stop being hungry all the time.

The problem is that they have, from the very beginning, talked themselves into being unsuccessful. They let life take them where it may (like a victim) because that is what their friends told them has to happen. They throw clutter out into the world and wait passively to catch someone's eye and get their lucky break.

I'm certainly not trying to claim that every starving artist is doomed, just like I'm not claiming that your friends are the only way to find your ultimate success. I'm definitely not making the claim that there is no chance of success for these artists if they spend their time in these groups or at the events. I am saying that there are other routes and groups with higher possibilities of success available. Remember how I mentioned at the start that there are a select group of extremely talented individuals who make the right choices, have a touch of luck and make it to the all exclusive There while following these traditional methods. As I mentioned in earlier chapters, those occasional successes are the only encouragement everyone else needs to stay on that path. But with as many starving artists as exist in the world today, and how few actually make it to the fame and fortune they are looking for, wouldn't you rather increase your likelihood of success by putting yourself in a position to meet people and expose yourself to the right circumstances that can elevate you exponentially?

Yes, it is a selfish decision to make to some extent, but bear in mind that I'm not telling you to abandon your friends. Just be aware that there is a romantic lure in the starving artist title and many of those who follow it don't have the background necessary to help you escape it. Often just putting yourself in the position to meet others who have achieved what you want, repeatedly, can change your mindset and worldview enough to help you view your efforts differently and help you realign yourself with a route to success that has a higher, no pun intended, success rate.

Let me give you an example. Take a painter who has been exhibiting his art at local Starbucks'® and on the local First Friday Art Walk religiously. He puts it all online in all the right places like his friends told him to do, walks around with the characteristic artist look of paint on his hands and a haunted look in his eyes and meets with his friends at least weekly to bemoan how people don't appreciate good art enough to pay for it.

In this example, unless his art is somehow good enough and new enough and different enough to break through the overwhelming circus of colors and attention hogs out there, the likelihood that he'll break into his own gallery or end up with his own show is extremely slim. Let's say, for the sake of this example, that this same talented young painter spends his spare time attending local galleries and art museums and makes an effort to meet the people who make these locations work and learn about them. In the process he finds a friend who is willing to give him a leg up to get his own show or introduce him to those who can make the show happen. In this new arena of friends, the painter begins to learn what these people did to achieve the success they are enjoying and figures out how to apply it in his life too. Do you see how the second scenario could easily lead to a gallery owner offering to show off the artist's work or making the much needed to connection to build his reputation?

I'm not promising that it will always work out like that, but which scenario do you think has the better chance at succeeding in getting the artist a full-time career in his field that pays, and pays well? The one who spends his time sipping coffee and complaining to his friends about how no one touches his paintings because the world is so jaded and shallow that they just don't understand him. Or the one who surrounds himself with those who have achieved at least some measure of the success he is craving and can provide guide lines to help him grow?

I want to clarify once again that being a starving artist isn't a final destination for all starving artists and for some creators, it truly is just a phase in their lives. These gifted individuals will make it to bigger and better and bolder things in the realm of their chosen field (usually through a "lucky break" with the friends that they've chosen). However, that's not the case for most of these artists and those are the ones I am talking about here.

Chapter 14
The Passionist v. The Hobbiest

The all-elusive They, and most of the financially affluent folk in the world, say that if you do what you love, you'll never work a day in your life and most of them manage to make excellent money following that advice. Yet there also seems to be a substantial lack of people who are able to make a living doing what they love. There are more and more people who are going to work every day at a job they hate to pay the bills and leaving what should be their passion to the hobby-hours (after or before work). If it's truly possible to find what you love, look for a way to market or profit from it, and find the right people to spend time around until greatness is forced on you, what is the secret missing ingredient holding people back from making their hobbies their full-time jobs?

More often than not it's lack of dedication which, you guessed it, stems from the company they keep. Those who have a hobby rarely intend for their hobbies to support them, so while they may dream about it and make passing comments about how wonderful it would be, there is dedication missing from the equation. These hobbies are confined to a few hours of the weekend, after-work hours, or even treated as an occasional treat once or twice a month. Even for those who feel that they started the hobby passionate about making it into a full-time career, many have lost the driving fire that started their idealistic plunge and they are trying to cook a steak on coals that are barely flickering, then wondering why there's no sizzle. They've gotten caught up in the mundane activity of their hobby and are just enjoying the experience rather than evaluating and learning ways to grow and build and surrounding themselves with others successful passionists. It doesn't consume their lives and so it will never support their lives.

In some cases, there are hobbies that, for whatever reasons, aren't ready to be turned into full-time jobs. But if you're sitting here, reading this chapter and shaking your head, pursing your lips and calling me foolish take a moment and think back on your past and your most recent emotions. Have you truly, earnestly, with every fiber in your being wanted it to become what you do for a living? Has there been hesitation when you look at that possibility and you're bombarded by the thoughts of how you'll handle it, or how you don't want it to become work because you'll hate doing it? Now think about how many people you are regularly and avidly spending your time with that have turned your hobby into a full-time job? I would be nearly willing to bet that the answer to that second question is zero.

More often than not, there's too many problems to overcome, or because there is so much dislike for his or her job, the hobbiest doesn't truly want to make their hobby into a full-time career because he or she doesn't want it to become as hateful as a job often can be. So instead, the hobbiests spend their time griping and complaining because they don't have enough time in the day to devote to the hobby or daydreaming about how wonderful it would be to spend their time on that hobby. It's very rare that a hobbiest has chosen a role-model who has made a profession out of the hobby and if there is, it's even rarer that the hobbiest has made it a priority to meet that role model. It is almost beyond belief that the hobbiest would have tried to become friends with the role model or asked them to coach or mentor the hobbiest to success.

Most of all, these hobbiest are so busy complaining that they never receive recognition for the efforts of their passion that they forget that they are surrounded by a world of talented people. In his book *Outliers: The Story of Success*, Malcolm Gladwell states that it takes 10,000 hours of practice to achieve mastery of something and points to proof in the lives not only of the most elite musicians in a German study but also in the lives of many famously successful individuals such as Bill Gates and the Beatles. Most hobbiests have invested a tenth of that time at most. In order to get paid better than anyone in your field, you have to have a reason to get paid better – either produce or perform better, or make the right connections. First and foremost, if you're looking for your hobby to support your life, you need to make that decision 100% and head in that direction without reservations. Too many people live under the assumption that it's not possible to do what you love and get paid well. I have a revelation for you, when you dedicate yourself to an outcome 100%, a vehicle to get yourself to that outcome will show up. I'm living proof of this.

Next, be willing to immerse yourself in what you want to take over your life. When you immerse yourself in your passion, you will find yourself spending more and more time with those who have achieved your version of ultimate success. It's a natural progression to, once an idea begins to consume your life, surround yourself with one of two kinds of people: the wannabes or the professionals. If you want to be a wannabe, spend your time there. If you want to be a professional, take my advice and put yourself in that situation instead.

I have a lot of quotes that I feel really embody this concept but there is one that I heard quite some time ago that really struck me, "You will rise to the level of your peer group." I would only modify that quote to mention "or sink."

For the sake of showcasing both pieces of Friend Power in this arena, take this scenario. An older gentleman who has a passion that many people consider a hobby: model boat building. He spends hours every week on his boats. For the sake of our story, we'll pretend he is exceptionally talented and his boats are large, detailed piece of art. In this scenario, he spends several hours each week on his boats, amid golfing and family time and has blissful dreams of his boats selling for thousands of dollars and all the things he could do with the money in his retirement and his boats being a masterpiece exhibited in all the financially affluent homes across America.

In order to help his dream come true, he rents a booth at a local hobby show and sets his boats up on display. The event results may vary, but in the first version of this example, our protagonist is so eager to sell boats that he barely talks to the other booth holders around him and brought only his best and highest quality boats and the sales are far below his rosy projections. On the off chance he makes an effort to talk to the booth owners around him he'll hear one of two stories "You're right, no one is buying and this show is a waste of time" or "I don't know what to tell you, this has been a great show for us!"

Now imagine a slightly altered scenario. Our hero spends hours working on building his boats, but he also spends hours at the local hobby shop and around other craftsmen. Because he is passionate about these boats, he's working on them with a fever and running to the hobby shop at least once every other week to get supplies and he strikes up a friendship with the hobby-shop owner. The owner, in turn, begins to hold special supplies for him, cuts deals on supplies and eventually mentions that he should take his boats to a home décor event going on the following month. The shop owner in all likelihood (assuming that this is a shop that is thriving and not one on the brink of bankruptcy) will know someone else who has used these types of shows before, may even be at the upcoming show and can provide advice on what kind of audience to expect, what kinds of boats (and prices) will be best to bring and how to style his booth to get the most interest.

In that second scenario, you could replace the hobby shop owner with a designer or with someone who makes a living selling high-end décor. Both of these potential connections are in a place to know what it takes to make a living out of what they love, and can help our protagonist connect with the right shows and the right people while avoiding the pitfalls that might otherwise take him down completely. These types of people, however, will only exert themselves to make that connection for a friend and someone they want to help.

In both of these cases, there was one driving difference: the passion of the hobbiest. His determination and passion for his craft drove him to spend much longer hours encased in the art and brought him back to the store more often where he got to make more connections. His passion and the connections he made makes the difference in turning a hobby into a money-making reality.

This chapter is really supposed to have cemented two main ideas in your head. First, don't expect to skate by on just who you know – our hobbiest still had to have excellent quality in his work – but that quality doesn't guarantee him a place in the limelight. Second, who you know has influence over much more of your life than you might have originally thought.

Chapter 15
Athletic Superiority Isn't Everything

What does it take to make it to athletic superiority? I'm not talking about fit and in-shape. I'm talking about the kind of athletic superiority that results in millions of dollars in sponsors through the Olympics or a multi-million dollar contract with the NFL. If you've been paying attention to the rest of this book, I'd hope that it's pretty self-evident that I'm about to promote the company you surround yourself and the friends you create as a portion of that equation. Just like the rest of our examples, there is a heavy reliance on your own capability. I, for example, will never be an all-star quarterback in the NFL, even if I make all the right connections and all the right friends (before someone sends me a letter about mindset, let me clarify this by stating that I have hardly any interest in the NFL outside of the joy it brings to my significant other). As always, if you really want to find success in your quest for athletic superiority, the company you surround yourself will play heavily into how easily you succeed.

Just to be clear, once again, I am not talking about your skill level. Again, the kind of athletic superiority I'm talking about requires intense skill, talent and drive. I'm talking about NFL levels in football, Olympic levels in swimming or US Congress levels in horseback riding. In order to compete at these levels, skill must be off the charts and while the company you keep may keep you focused enough to stay there, I'm focused a little more in this chapter about how your friend power can help you arrive at these levels.

Think for just a minute to how many NFL players made it to the NFL by attending a school with a mediocre football team and no track record of excellence or family history in the NFL? How many talented athletes have ever made it to the Olympics without a coach? While I am sure there are exceptions to the general rule – just as in every category – the vast majority of our great success stories have surrounded themselves with a team of people to make them effective. Without a coach or a mentor who has experience in the levels you want to achieve, it's extremely difficult to break through to serious success.

For the sake of argument, and because it's the arena I'm most familiar with, let's make our example athlete a young equestrian. For this scenario, we'll say that our equestrian's ultimate success is to compete on the US Olympic Dressage team. She's extremely passionate about riding, incredibly talented and watching her ride is magical. Her connection with her horse is unreal. She doesn't just ride her horse around the arena, together they dance. She harbors dreams of being found by a scout at the shows she attends and has a wall full of ribbons. Horses are everything in her life and her long-term goal is to build a professional horse-training business to rival Monty Roberts. She's young and focused, riding regularly and showing regularly. Yet years go by and no scouts pick her out of the crowd to sweep her away and bring her to the Olympic Dressage team.

Eventually, life gets in the way. Relationships develop with significant others and at work that begin to pull at her time. Blissful afternoons at the barn get relocated to weekend events, then twice a month, fewer and further between the more time she spends with co-workers, significant others, and family. Plans and goals simply shifted. While her passion was high, she wasn't able to get the break she needed to make it into a perfect career and so it slowly fades into the background. Even if everyone she spends her time with encourages her to continue with the horses, the company she's kept has changed that focus. Without a coach and a strong support system to keep her grounded in her equine work, it will fall by the wayside.

More than just the grounding in her interests to keep her passion high, unless she can find a coach who knows what it takes to break into the arena of Olympic level riders, she is leaving her success up to dumb luck to be found by a scout. How would she possibly know which shows to attend or what trials to participate in? On top of that, it doesn't matter how good raw talent is, without someone who has an eye to hold that talent accountable to the proper levels of perfection, pushing into Olympic levels of quality will be nearly impossible.

In this scenario, our rider needs to make a conscious effort to stay surrounded by other equine-enthusiasts and keep herself in a regular showing circuit. It's also imperative that she finds a coach who has experience in those levels of success. Without that coach she's going to be fighting a very up-hill battle and making all the same mistakes over and over that others have learned not to make if they want to achieve success.

On the same thread as athletic superiority, one of the most famous national sports in the USA, football, has a history of friend power easing the way into the upper leagues. There are more than a couple leading players who have a history riddled with NFL experience and success. Many players have fathers and grandfathers who played for the NFL or attended highly-renowned, football-driven schools. While a lot of their success and fame has come from their drive and their talent, there is an element that provides them with the opening to share their talent with the world that hinges on the people they've surrounded themselves with.

I can state it a hundred different ways, but it still comes down to the simple truth that having people who have achieved some level of the success you're searching for as the people you keep closest to you makes a difference. Often times the wisdom they can offer gives you the edge you need to find your success. If they can't offer wisdom, they should be keeping your head in the right place at the very least.

Friend power makes it substantially easier to find your success. Think of it like someone opening the door for you. It's still your responsibility to walk through and go somewhere once you get to the other side, but instead of blindly searching for a door in the wall, you have someone to put you in the right position to find your door quickly.

Chapter 16
Victims Are Victims

Have you ever heard the phrase "birds of a feather flock together?" It's true. People hang out with like-minded people because it adds a feeling of normalcy to their lives. As I mentioned in chapter four we are all telling ourselves some kind of story about our lives. Everything we see, all the interactions we have, all the observations we make are done through the lens of the story we tell ourselves because it makes us feel better about ourselves and the stories we are telling.

This means that victims seek out other victims both consciously and sometimes subconsciously. This also means that victims, and really all humans, don't want the other person's story to change. As soon as your story changes, we won't necessarily get along as well and might stop hanging out – which destabilizes the story I tell myself as the one true story in the world. Because of that subconscious mindset, victims in particular will often make steps to keep others on the same level. The crab trap surfaces again.

Truthfully, many with the victim mentality not only take every excuse possible to be a victim but everything untoward that happens in their lives serves to cement the fact that, in their minds, they are a victim of life and the world is out to get them. For these individuals, life doesn't happen for them, it happens do them. It is hard to break that mindset because every little problem that arises for them is clearly, in their minds, occurring because of the way the world is set against them. You can see how this would perpetuate itself.

These people spend their time and energy only seeing the problems you encounter, pointing them out to you, and then trying to tell you that it's not your fault and you can't do anything about it. I'm sure you know who I am talking about: those who believe that life happens to you and you have no hand in it. Unfortunately, they really can't help it – that is all they see in their own lives as well. It takes an extraordinary person to rise above the victim mentality. Particularly because most people don't have the drive to do so. They are comfortable as a victim and they (perversely enough) enjoy the attention being a victim gets them. Because they are so focused on being a victim, they have no control over their own life and they are happiest that way. At least, they believe they are, often because they don't know any other way to live.

The problem is, the more you focus on something, the more it tends to happen to you (the law of attraction), so as victims spend time with victims and focus on being victims, then complain about being victims, they are finding more and more ways to be a victim!

Please don't get me wrong. There are plenty of heroic people who have undergone a horrible tragedy – kidnapping, rape, war, abuse, etc – and due to the nature of their experience do have an actual claim on the term victim. These are not the victims I am talking about. Most of the time, when you hear the stories of the above survivors, there is a line about how that person refuses to be a victim of what happened to them and we, as a society, embrace them for that tenacity. We love to hear about these people who have overcome serious odds and admire the person who can undergo a horrific tragedy and come out still positive. These are the genuine victims. The few who have dealt with something so very terrible that it is a true testament to their character that they are still standing, much less trying to get past that victim mentality. I am not here to belittle them.

I say this because I don't want to be misunderstood with this chapter. I know, firsthand, that there are those who struggle to get past what they experienced and I would never belittle those people by trying to claim it is their own fault that any of that happened to them. I don't make the claim that it is their own fault that they struggled with that or that they wanted that to happen them to give them an excuse to be a victim. Most of the victims I am talking about are not actually masochistic enough to want something truly terrible to happen to them.

In this chapter I am talking about the wannabe victims. The ones who would rather group around the water cooler or the smoke-room at work and gripe about how the world is set against them than take strides to fix it. The ones complaining and swapping stories about the troubles they are dealing with and how if it's not one thing it's another. There always seems to be a contest among these people: who can tell the most miserable story. I would know – I hung out with them for a few years. These workers (and I use workers but they are in every walk of life! Insert your title of preference as needed) hang out with each other because they edify each other for being miserable and being the butt of every joke and the scape goat around the office or at home. They build up each other's stories about the miserable existence of a life pitted against them.

Whether you realize it or not, as a victim you are always on the lookout for a better story to top everyone else. It's human nature to want to be better. If your peers are focusing on their problems, you'll focus on your problems so you can have a bigger problem than they do and somehow you are the winner in that situation. I hope you can pick up on the sarcasm in that twisted logic.

The lure is that, if you're struggling as well, these people make you feel marginally better and they make each other feel better. Sometimes they even convince themselves that they are telling the stories so they can laugh about it and get over it. The problem is that spending time dwelling on the difficulties that they are struggling against isn't helping anyone. If you've never had a chance to check it out, I highly recommend you look up the book (or the movie) *The Secret*. While the book itself (again) isn't a Bible and could require a whole conversation about its flaws and strengths, it does talk heavily about the concept of the law of attraction and that what you focus on expands. So when you focus on the problem rather than a solution, the problem overtakes your entire life. The more you focus on your problems, the more you will find bigger and bigger problems to conquer and since you're always looking for the problem, you stop looking for the solution or appreciating the lessons you learned in the midst of the crisis or the growth it triggered.

This is why it's so easy to stay a victim. First you've spent too much time thinking about it, then you've surrounded yourself with friends who validate your problems and encourage you by explaining it away and labeling any escapees Abnormal. At this point, you've mired yourself in such a bitter mindset that it's all you think about and when someone offers you a way out, you have a thousand excuses as to why it won't work.

In order to break free from that victim mentality, you first have to realize that you are in control of your own life. That is not something you will hear from other victims. If you want to get past your problems, you need to find people who do not allow themselves to be victims of life. You need to surround yourself with people who stand tall, hold the reins firmly and control their own destiny. There is a great quote from Irene C. Kassorla: "The pen that writes your life story must be held in your own hand." Unfortunately, if you spend all your time with people who believe that life is something that happens to you, you will never get Irene's idea through your head and pick up the pen to write your own story.

Chapter 17
How to Leverage Friend Power

I hope the topics in this book have been enlightening. If you find yourself feeling uncertain about how to proceed and take advantage of the ideas I've presented, this is the chapter you've been looking for. This is the chapter that will move you towards your ultimate success.

If, for some reason, you are feeling overwhelmed after reading this book I'd like to encourage you right now. It's not hard to break the Everyman Mold and smash the glass ceiling that has held you back from achieving the great success you aspire to. Want to know how I can say that with such confidence? You're reading this book. When I started writing this in 2013, I had multiple books I'd worked on and none of them had ever come remotely close to publication. I had no idea how to publish a book, or even finish a book, must less get a cover picture designed or get that book into people's hands.

The difference now is that I spent a long time surrounding myself with people who have not only published books, but taken them to best seller status. I reached out to the one man I knew who had taken not one, not two, but seven books to best seller status and got his help and feedback. I decided, not long after coming to my conclusions in 2013, that writing and publishing a book would be an excellent way to test my theory. I had no connections at the time with anyone who had ever published a book and actually gotten it into the hands of more than a few close friends and family members. When I decided that I wanted to write a self-help, success book, I realized very quickly that I needed to practice what I was preaching and surround myself with those who have achieved the success I dreamed of. In the process of writing this book, I discovered so much more success than I'd ever known and the journey has been more valuable than anything else.

I found my success through taking action. I took action by finding friends in successful authors and by writing this book. I took action to seek out and get to know successful people and some of those people turned out to be successful, published authors. I took action to build a business from scratch. Obviously, I am a huge proponent of taking action to achieve your ultimate success. The friends you make and the people you constantly surround yourself with are the ones who will keep your mindset right and keep encouraging you to take action, but ultimately that is up to you. You can read all the right books, you can surround yourself with all the right people, but sooner or later if you insist on staying as an action talker versus an action taker, those action-oriented, success-oriented friends will drift away. Why? Because they, even if it's only subconsciously, understand the power of the company that they surround themselves with and they don't have room in their lives for someone who is going to give them excuses to avoid taking action.

All that said, I realized that I needed a chapter in this book to give you steps to take for those of you seriously interested in making a change and leveraging Friend Power to achieve your ultimate success. I wanted a way to give you information to get past your invisible barriers and find your sweet victory.

The most important step in breaking through your barriers to attain your success is to wrap your mind around what I glanced at in chapter three: what do you want? What is your version of ultimate success? When I work with coaching clients this is the hardest step to overcome but also the single most important step. Like I discussed earlier, what you plan for, you will achieve. The simple truth is that if you plan to create success in certain arenas, and put together a good plan, you will find that friends in that area are attracted to you and you will generally find a way to make it happen. Being aware of the friends you choose can make it happen sooner rather than waiting for them to come find you. However, if you spend your time randomly wishing and daydreaming about success, but never take time to determine what exactly your ultimate success is, you'll flounder about trying to achieve some vague definition and never arrive.

For example, when we talked about our hobbiest in chapter fourteen, the one who wanted to be the most highly valued builder of model boats in the world, it would be incredibly easy for him to struggle his whole life and never realize how close he got to achieving his goals. If, instead, he set a measurable counter to know when he's achieved his goals, he has an end to strive towards. Instead of wanting to be the most highly valued builder, it would be a better motivator to choose something measurable: being featured in the home and décor collector's edition of their magazine and to be a featured artist in x, y and z shops. In this second case, he has a goal and a goal he will know when he achieves. He can find people who have achieved that goal or a similar one and do his best to replicate their success.

Likewise if you want to become a leader in your company, a body builder or an athlete you must know what success looks like so you will know when you arrive. Is it the promotion to regional manager? Taking gold at the regional body building competition? Getting chosen for the US Olympic team? If you want to find success in your own business, you need to know what kind of business you are striving for and determine what success looks like in your industry and for you. Like I said earlier, there are a lot of people who are in love with the notion of being a starving artist and who find it easier to play the victim than to struggle to overcome the world. Who do you want to be? I encourage you to write it down and keep it in front of you daily.

When you've decided who you want to be, now it's time to find the right people to spend your time with. If your dream needs the support of a community that concentrates in a specific city, don't be afraid to go for it. If you want to be a country singer, you might consider moving to Nashville, or Los Angeles if you want to become a movie actor or New York if you want theater. If your chief goal in life is to become a famous surfer, it might be time to head to Hawaii.

I encourage you to be willing to put out some money to be in the right networking communities. If you are determined to be financially wealthy, you need to spend time at the events and locations where the wealthy congregate (country club stereotypes exist for a reason). Pay attention to the people you see every day, friendships don't always happen all at once, just like relationships, sometimes they take a little work. Don't be afraid to put that work in if you truly want that person in your life.

My next piece of encouragement is to inspire you to take one step every single day. If networking is hard for you, like it was for me at first, force yourself to meet one new person every day. Spend time getting to know them instead of just learning their name and moving on. The people behind you in the grocery story, the clerk helping you, the librarian are all feasible connections and you'll never know the power they could wield over your life until you get to know them. I stir you to walk into that art gallery you're interested in being featured in and spend time chatting with the first person you meet there. Attend a runway show or a fashion class if that's your passion. Visit nutrition stores and chat with other fitness-buffs. You are the only person who knows your goals, so you are the only person who can consider what kinds of people you need to surround yourself with to make them come true. Once you know the kinds of people you need to meet, you can find a list of places that they occupy.

One concern I hear regularly from coaching clients is that they might change their mind. Right now, this goal is perfect, but what if their goals change over the year? Isn't it better to wait until they know what they want and then start moving forward so that they don't waste energy? In this case, wouldn't it be harmful to surround yourself with friends to support one goal if you later decide you want to pursue another? My advice is always the same: you burn less gas turning the wheel and changing direction than you do getting to 60 miles per hour. It takes a lot of energy to get momentum going towards your success. If your goals change, you will naturally begin to adjust your friends, but you will never start towards creating success in your life unless you start somewhere.

Now I come to the last action step I can offer and the hardest part of this whole concept. Cut the dead weight. Stop hanging out with people who fit your old lifestyle. They won't understand and they will try to drag you back into your old life. Remember that those people, in the goodness of their hearts, don't want things to change for you because change isn't always a good or easy thing to them (crabs in a trap). So they will, even with the best intentions, hold you back and pull you under. They don't want to be left behind by you and the only way they can make sure that doesn't happen is to make sure you don't change.

If you want your success enough, strive for it and don't be afraid to spend less and less time with the people holding you back. If those people are truly important to you, have a conversation with them, help them become as dedicated to your success as you are. Otherwise, I suggest you start making plans to avoid spending as much time with those people and determine what you will replace that experience with. Very little happens unless you plan for it, so make your plans! Plan for success. Decide if what you want is worth going for it, and make it happen.

Chapter 18
Conclusions

Jim Rohn once said that you become a merging of the five people you spend the most time with. He goes on to caution you to choose your five wisely. I do the same. For some people, it's too late to choose all of your five. Spouses should always be in that top five, and most of the time have the most influence on who you will become. I'm hopeful that you can at least be aware of the sway that your spouse has on you and make it work to your best advantage.

I want to state one last time that I am not condoning using and manipulating friends to get what you want or to use them and leave them. I encourage people to, instead, cultivate friendships. You can't be friends with someone you are using and abusing. You put effort and care and love into a friendship just like into a garden and you will never get the full effect of the power of your friends if you are looking to only connect with people who can help you and you can use to achieve your goals. Instead, this book is about awareness as you build reciprocal relationships that use a constant give and take and choosing friends that won't pull you down. This book is about putting yourself in positions to find friends who will lift you up and you can lift up and enjoy spending time with.

The idea of making friends with someone only to take advantage of their knowledge or connections completely undermines the concept of Friend Power by assuming that those people only have one or two things to offer you or you have nothing to offer them in return. I also don't condone breaking your commitments. Familial relationships are not ones you can necessarily walk away from (although that's a whole different book) and if you have committed to spending time with someone, it's important to fulfill your commitments. But be aware of the power that is created in that relationship and find a way to use it to your advantage. It's essential to realize that you do not have to share everything with everyone. The people who won't lift you up and encourage you to follow your dreams don't need to know everything and they don't need to be in your top five. The people who will eagerly tear you down and pull you back into the crab trap of life don't have to be a big part of your life and it is okay to hide your dreams from those who won't help you out.

One of the strongest reasons I propone using friend power to give yourself an advantage is nicely summed up in Napoleon Hill's *Think & Grow Rich*. "Too many of those who begin at the bottom never manage to lift their heads high enough to be seen by opportunity so they remain at the bottom. ... The outlook from the bottom is not so very bright or encouraging. It has a tendency to kill off ambition." I know this from experience. It took a major encounter at a weekend seminar to break the blinders I'd picked up after only two years of working in corporate America. I'd begun to believe the lies I've outlined in this book. When you give yourself leverage to skip a few steps through the power of your friends, you make it substantially easier to avoid falling into the rut that kills so many of the American dreams.

Tony Robbin's once asked "what if life isn't happening to you but happening for you?" I encourage you to think about that now and give yourself permission to dream of what you could do with your life if you embrace that concept and decide to make a difference starting with the friends you choose. Remember how I talked about the difference between action takers and action talkers in chapter five (and again and again throughout the rest of the book)? Now is a good time to go back and re-read that chapter and remember the power of action takers surrounded by action takers, or even an action talker who forces him or herself to be surrounded by action takers.

I've always been told that there is payment due, no matter what you choose to do with your life and that there is both a cost and a reward to taking action. There's a time and energy investment you need to make to adjust your friends and start changing your thinking and mindset to achieve your goals and dreams and start taking action.

There is also a cost to leaving yourself in the situation you're currently in and that is all the pain, grief and frustration you'll experience by not stepping out and making the changes you know you need to make right now. The choice is yours.

The friends you choose can change the course of your life.

My Favorite Non-Fiction Reading Material:

10X Rule by Grant Cardone
All Marketers ~~Are Liars~~ Tell Stories by Seth Godin
Awaken the Giant Within by Tony Robbins
Blink by Malcolm Gladwell
Bulls Eye by Eric Lofholm
How I Raised Myself from Failure to Success in Selling by Frank Bettger
Money: Master the Game by Tony Robbins
Outliers by Malcolm Gladwell
Rich Dad, Poor Dad by Robert Kiyosaki
Secrets of The Millionaire Mind by T. Harv Ecker
The Magic of Thinking Big by David J. Schwartz
The Secret by Rhonda Byrnes
The Strangest Secret by Earl Nightingale
The System by Eric Lofholm
The Tipping Point by Malcolm Gladwell
Think & Grow Rich by Napoleon Hill

About the Author:

Stephanie Scheller is a dynamic speaker and writer with eleven years of public speaking behind her and a lifetime of sales acumen! She has been writing since before she could form letters by scribbling wavy on stolen printer paper and loves pouring her thoughts onto paper. She has consistently been a top performer in her career and is passionate about sales, business and creating your ultimate success.